creepy creatures

CONTENTS

Published by Creative Education
P.O. Box 227, Mankato, Minnesota 56002
Creative Education is an imprint of
The Creative Company
www.thecreativecompany.us

Design and production by Ellen Huber
Art direction by Rita Marshall
Printed by Corporate Graphics
in the United States of America

Photographs by 123RF (Joao Estevao, David Good,
Adrian Hillman, Pavel Konovalov, Christian Musat, Oleksiy),
Corbis (Asian Art & Archaeology, Inc.), CritterZone.com
(Andrew Williams, Wim Acke), Getty Images (George
Grall), iStockphoto (Evgeniy Ayupov, Adam Gryko, Eric
Isselée, Renee Lee, Gary Milner, Morley Read), Jim A.
Rowan Photography, Shutterstock (Anton Chemenko,
Robert Adrian Hillman), Superstock (Age Fotostock)

Library of Congress Cataloging-in-Publication Data
Bodden, Valerie.
Centipedes / by Valerie Bodden.
p. cm. — (Creepy creatures)
Summary: A basic introduction to centipedes,
examining where they live, how they grow, what
they eat, and the unique physical traits that help to
define them, such as their numerous pairs of legs.
Includes index.
ISBN 978-1-58341-992-2
1. Centipedes—Juvenile literature. I. Title. II. Series.
QL449.5.B63 2011
595.6'2—dc22   2009052516
CPSIA: 040110 PO1135

First Edition
9 8 7 6 5 4 3 2 1

centipedes

VALERIE BODDEN

CREATIVE 🍎 EDUCATION

You are in your
basement when you
spot a strange-looking
creature scurrying
across the floor.
You bend down
to take a closer look.
The creature has
lots of legs.

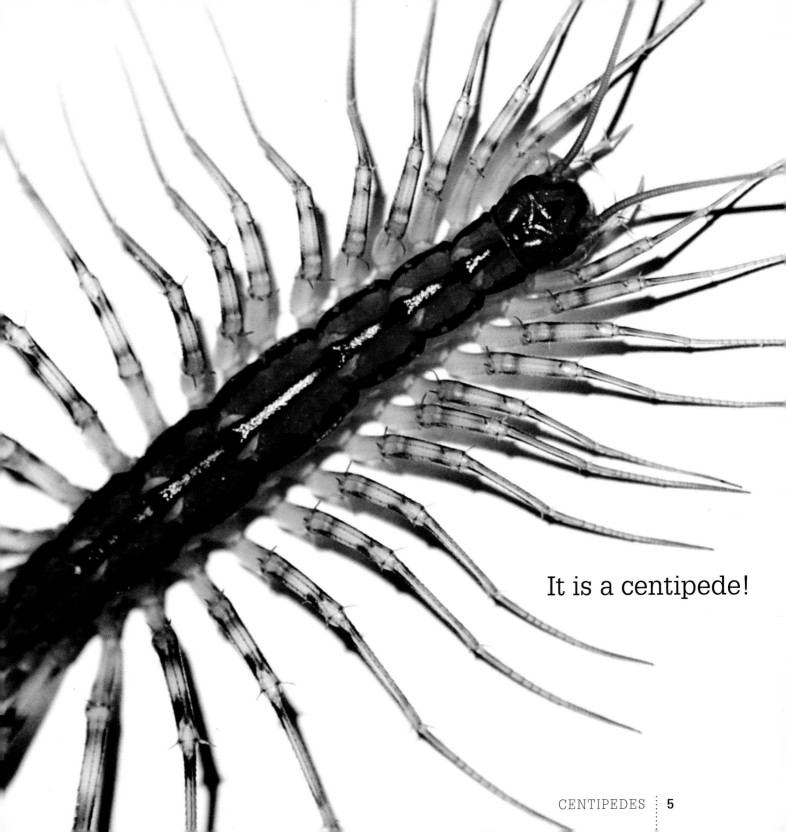

It is a centipede!

Centipedes have lots of legs on their bendy bodies

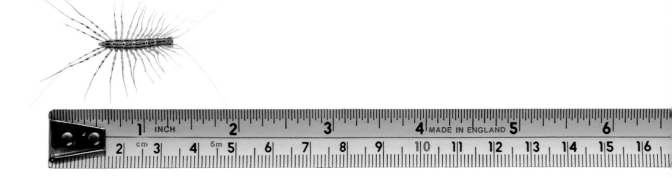

Centipedes are **arthropods**. Most centipedes are about one or two inches (2.5–5 cm) long. But some can grow as long as a ruler! Some centipedes have 30 legs. Others have more than 350!

Centipedes have bad eyesight and use their antennae to "see" things

A centipede's head has two antennae (*an-TEH-nee*). The antennae help the centipede touch, smell, and taste things.

Centipedes have two **poisonous** claws on
their body behind their head. Most centipedes
are yellow, brown, or red.

There are more than 2,500 different kinds of centipedes. House centipedes can be found in many people's homes. Soil centipedes and stone centipedes are common kinds of centipedes, too.

Most centipedes stay outside on trees or stones

Most centipedes live where it is warm. They make their homes in deserts, forests, and grasslands. Centipedes have to watch out for **predators**. Birds, spiders, and lizards all eat centipedes.

Wolf spiders and green lizards eat centipedes

Most mother centipedes lay about 40 eggs. Baby centipedes look like small adult centipedes. As they grow, the centipedes get too big for their skin. They **molt** so they can keep growing. Some centipedes live for five years.

Mother centipedes keep their eggs close to their bodies

Most centipedes eat **insects**, spiders, and worms. Big centipedes can eat frogs, too! Centipedes hunt for food at night. When they find an animal to eat, they stab it with their poisonous claws.

Bugs, tree frogs, and some spiders can be centipede food

Some centipedes can play a special trick. If another animal is going to attack them, they can make some of their legs fall off. The legs that fall off keep wiggling. The animal looks at the wiggling legs while the centipede runs away!

Some centipedes are brightly colored

to keep other creatures away from them

Long ago, people in Egypt thought that one of their **gods** looked like a centipede. People in Japan told stories about heroes fighting giant centipedes. It can be fun finding and watching these many-legged creepy creatures!

This picture from Japan shows a man hunting a giant centipede

MAKE A CENTIPEDE

You can make your own centipede with a Popsicle stick and some yarn!

First, paint your Popsicle stick red, brown, or yellow.

Have a grown-up help you cut your yarn into 15 or 20 pieces, each about 1 inch (2.5 cm) long.

When the paint on your Popsicle stick has dried, glue the middle of each piece of yarn to the bottom of the stick. Now your centipede has lots of legs!

GLOSSARY

arthropods: animals with a body that has different parts called segments and that is covered by a hard shell

gods: beings that people think have special powers and control the world

insects: small animals with three body parts and six legs; most have two pairs of wings, too

molt: to lose a shell or layer of skin and grow a new, larger one

poisonous: filled with something that can hurt or kill other animals or people if it gets into their body

predators: animals that kill and eat other animals

READ MORE

Dickmann, Nancy. *Centipedes*. Chicago: Raintree, 2006.

Hall, Margaret. *Centipedes*. Mankato, Minn.: Capstone Press, 2006.

WEB SITES

Enchanted Learning: Centipede
http://www.enchantedlearning.com/subjects/invertebrates/arthropod/Centipede.shtml
Learn more about centipedes and print a centipede picture to color.

The Field Museum Underground Adventure: Meet the Creepy Critters
http://www.fieldmuseum.org/underground adventure/critters/critter_info.shtml
Read fun facts about centipedes.